ABOVE AND

LIGHTHOUSES AND SHIPWRECKS OF ISLE ROYALE

by Thom Holden

Isle Royale Natural History Association
Houghton, Michigan 49931

CONTENTS

Introduction 1

Rock Harbor Lighthouse (1855) 2

ALGOMA (1883-1885) 5

Passage Island Lighthouse (1882) 10

MONARCH (1890-1906) 13

Blake Point Light (1917) 16

CHESTER A. CONGDON (1907-1918) 17

EMPEROR (1910-1947) 20

Isle Royale Lighthouse (1875) 23

GLENLYON (1893-1924) 25

KAMLOOPS (1924-1927) 28

Rock of Ages Lighthouse (1908) 32

CUMBERLAND (1871-1877) 36

HENRY CHISHOLM (1880-1898) 38

GEORGE M. COX (1901-1933) 41

AMERICA (1898-1928) 49

Other Shipwrecks 59

References 61

Acknowledgement 63

Lake Superior

DISTANCE IN MILES

0 1 2 3 4 5

Little Tod

Rock of Ages Lighthouse

America

Washington Harbor

Henry Chisholm

Cumberland

George M. Cox

Long Point

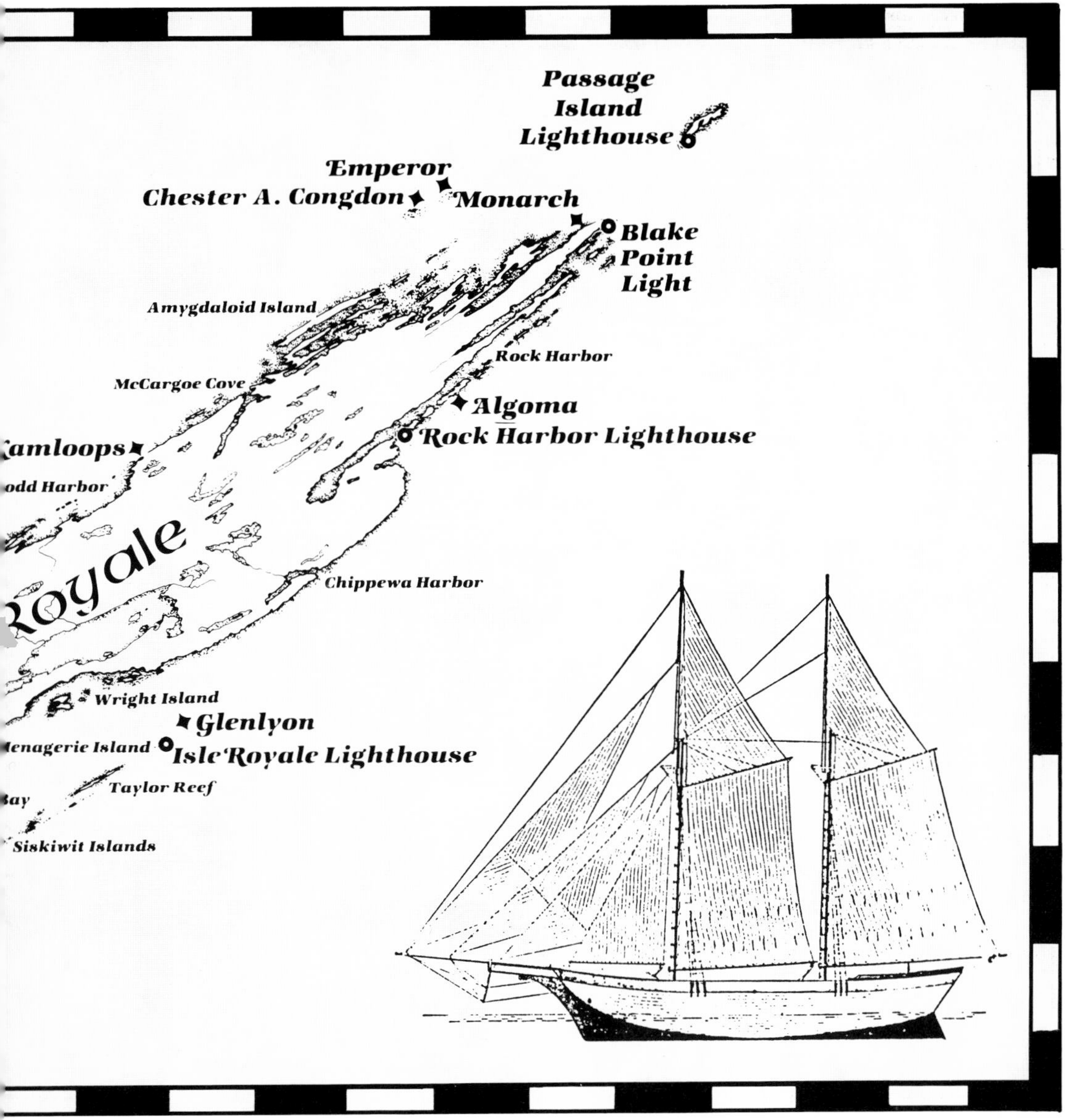

Passage Island Lighthouse

Emperor
Chester A. Congdon **Monarch**

Blake Point Light

Amygdaloid Island

Rock Harbor

McCargoe Cove

Algoma
Rock Harbor Lighthouse

Kamloops

odd Harbor

Royale

Chippewa Harbor

Wright Island

Glenlyon
Menagerie Island **Isle Royale Lighthouse**

Bay

Taylor Reef

Siskiwit Islands

INTRODUCTION

Born of fire and ice in the millenia of geologic times past, Isle Royale has become well known for its recreational opportunities and its seemingly endless array of animal and plant life. This special island's human history is another of its many intriguing aspects. For more than a century and a half, commercial fishing stations have dotted its extensive shoreline. Prospectors of the mid 1800s scoured its ridges for copper deposited here in nearly pure metallic form. And surrounding Isle Royale, beneath the cold blue waters of Lake Superior, are at least ten major shipwrecks marking past tragedies.

The "Song of the Sirens" beckoned more than 100 vessels with its alluring melody of misfortune to the rugged shores of Isle Royale, truly the "wilderness port" of Lake Superior. Some were lucky in breaking the spell while others made it their final port of call. Isle Royale's shipwreck history goes back at least to October 1840 when the small American Fur Company schooner *Siskawit* wrecked near its fishing and trapping station in Siskiwit Bay.

Today, there are 10 major shipwrecks within Isle Royale National Park which have been located, identified and explored. A few known casualties have yet to be located, and the possibility of discovering currently unknown shipwrecks still remains. Numerous small craft, many from the boom days of commercial fishing, literally ring the island, appearing in the shallows of her many bays and harbors.

Following is an account of the 10 major shipwrecks combined with brief histories of Isle Royale's five light stations. There are also glimpses of some of those vessels known to be lost at Isle Royale, but not located in recent times. The narratives are presented in roughly chronological order, beginning with the northeastern end of the island, going then to the south and north shore midsections and concluding with the southwestern end.

A complete history of any one of these accidents could easily fill this small volume. A bibliography is appended to assist in further exploration and discovery of this fascinating aspect of Isle Royale National Park's history and archeology--from above and below.

ROCK HARBOR LIGHTHOUSE (1855)

A treaty with the Chippewa Indians in 1843 opened Isle Royale to the first wave of modern copper mining exploration. The valuable red metal had been reported after 1837 when the first American Fur Company fishery was established here. A dozen or more copper companies had locations on the island by 1847. Together, pressures from the mining companies and commercial fisheries established a clear need for a lighthouse on Isle Royale to guide their supply vessels safely to and from the island.

A general location was chosen and a preliminary survey completed in 1847 for a lighthouse to be built near the southwestern entrance to Rock Harbor. Meanwhile, the anticipated 1855 opening of the locks at Sault Ste. Marie, Michigan, and the increased vessel traffic they would permit further emphasized the need for the lighthouse. Finally completed in 1855, Rock Harbor Lighthouse remains steadfast, marking Middle Islands Passage, although no longer illuminated.

The original lighthouse remained in use from 1855 to 1859 when the station was discontinued because mining exploration ceased. In response to pressure, Congress authorized the light to be rekindled in August 1874. This same year, there was renewed interest in mining, and the Saginaw Mine opened only a few miles away. The lamp was permanently extinguished at end-of-season in 1879 (only a year after the Saginaw Mine

ceased production) largely in deference to the more centrally located Isle Royale Light, established in 1875 on Menagerie Island.

For more than 100 years after the Rock Harbor Light last held its glow of safety aloft, the attached keeper's dwelling was used as a home by a series of commercial fishermen and at least one summer resident. Today, it is undergoing continued restoration and stabilization befitting its enrollment on the National Register of Historic Places. Tours of the lighthouse grounds and the nearby historic Edisen fishery are conducted regularly in summer by National Park Service interpreters.

Rock Harbor Lighthouse around 1900
From an old postcard
(C. Patrick Labadie Collection)

ALGOMA, with 1100 passengers on her maiden voyage, passed upbound through the Weitzel Lock at Sault Ste. Marie on May 12, 1884.
(Toronto Marine Historical Society Collection)

ALGOMA (1883-1885)

Not far distant from the Rock Harbor Light is the wreck of the *Algoma*. She was built in 1883 as one of three nearly identical sisters, the product of skilled Scottish shipbuilders and pride of the Canadian Pacific Railway (CPR) fleet. *Athabasca*, the first of the Clyde-built sister ships, was launched July 3, 1883, at Whiteinch. On July 12, 1883, the *Alberta* slid down the launchways at Scotstown. Last, the *Algoma* was launched by builders Aitken & Mansel at their Kelvinhaugh yard on July 31, 1883. The *Algoma* was a steel-hulled passenger liner outfitted in finest Victorian manner including electric lights throughout.

All three vessels were designed to carry 240 first-class passengers and 600 more in steerage below deck as well as handling a variety of package freight and occasionally bulk cargoes of grain. Each was 263.5 feet long, too long for transit through the Welland Canal at that time, so was designed to be cut in two for that passage, then reassembled and cabin work completed on Lake Erie above the Canal.

Each of the sisters set out across the Atlantic from Glasgow to Montreal, the *Athabasca* on September 3 carrying coal. She had been at sea 10 days earlier but returned with leaking boilers. *Alberta* cleared on September 10 with a similar cargo. *Algoma* cleared Glasgow on September 24 carrying general merchandise. Each was powered by a two-cylinder, 1700-horsepower steam engine.

Algoma arrived at Owen Sound on May 10, 1884, initiating passenger service the following day by carrying a record 1,100 passengers, some 260 in excess of her designer's expectations and far in excess of her lifesaving apparatus. She cleared the Soo Locks on May 12 arriving safely in Port Arthur the next day.

The *Algoma* and her sisters had been built to fill a gap in the CPR's passenger line by running from Owen Sound on Lake Huron to Port Arthur on Lake Superior. Passengers would then disembark for CPR's soon-to-be-completed transcontinental rail line. Coincidentally, the *Algoma* was lost on the exact day the last spike was driven to complete the railway. Subsequently, the Canadian Pacific Railway fleet proved to have a remarkably safe operating history, the only major casualty being the *Algoma*.

After two successful seasons, the *Algoma's* last voyage began on November 5, 1885, at Owen Sound under Captain John Moore. She was carrying 400 tons of general merchandise and about 51 persons, including crew, when she passed through the Soo Locks on the following day. She was expected in Port Arthur on the 7th. Above Whitefish Point, the *Algoma* encountered increasingly heavy weather and strong winds. Yet she forged ahead. Later, believing he was still about 15 miles off Isle Royale, Captain Moore ordered the *Algoma* turned into the open lake to ride out the storm there rather than risk "threading the needle" off Passage Island and again off Thunder Cape. Unfortunately, he had not fully compensated for the strong southeasterly tailwind that had driven the *Algoma* faster than expected and several miles off course.

ALGOMA's stern section, just a few days after
the accident, with sails still in the rigging and
the search party still looking for the lost.
(Thunder Bay Historical Society Collection)

The *Algoma* struck hard in the early morning darkness of November 7, 1885, just offshore of Mott Island. A full gale was blowing, and snow and sleet further reduced visibility. The *Algoma* was fast on the rocks and being battered unmercifully. Her hull split apart just forward of the engine room, the bow slipping off into deeper water. Waves ripped away the remaining cabin until the deck was swept clear, leaving only Captain Moore, 11 crewman, and two passengers to survive the ordeal. Captain Moore was later credited by all survivors with providing constant hope throughout those dreadful hours.

At first light the survivors could see the stern was only a short distance off the rocky beach. They reached shore on a makeshift raft where local fishermen cared for them until November 9, when they were able to flag down the *Athabasca*, which was headed toward the Soo Locks. The *Athabasca's* crew had been keeping a keen lookout for their sister, then two full days overdue. All were taken aboard the *Athabasca* and returned to Port Arthur. That same day Keeper John H. Malone of the Isle Royale Light on Menagerie Island made the following entry in his journal: "We saw pieces of the wreck of the *Algoma* in Siscowette Bay, Isle Royal. We picked up a uniform coat belonging to some of the officers on board the steamer *Algoma* wrecked at Rock Harbor. It layed 2 feet from the edge of the water and 7 miles from the wreck. It had in one of the pockets 14 first class tickets."

An inquiry into the casualty was held in January 1886 after Captain Moore had recovered sufficiently to testify. It determined that the *Algoma* was lost through overruning the estimated distance, traveling before the wind at nearly 16 miles per hour, and suggested that the accident might have been avoided if the taffrail log and lead line had been used. Subsequently, Captain Moore was found negligent and suspended for 12 months although this was shortened to nine months "owing to previous good record, and to the fact that he had pursued the usual custom in navigating the large lakes," that is, depending upon the magnetic compass, engine revolutions, clock and landmarks for navigation.

In the spring of 1886 before winter ice completely submerged the stern, salvage of the ship's engine and other equipment began. Keeper Malone made several entries of interest over that summer:

June 28: "We found 4 life preservers on the beach abreast of our station (Menagerie Island) belonging to the illfated steamer Algoma. They are damaged from washing along the Island. Also found a couple of small pieces of a piano--some wire mattras frames and one pillow"

August 5: "The wrecking tug George Hand of Algonac passed the station up the Bay after a crib that laid there for blocking for the boilers of the Algoma. Captain Manyman Waecker said he has the machinery all out of her and said he will finish in a few days."

August 10: "We discovered a tug on the Schooner Island Reef almost a wreck. I found her to be the George Hand of Algonac, Michigan, the tug that was wrecking the steamer Algoma at Rock Harbor.

Workmen examine **ALGOMA**'s stern to evaluate
the possibility of salvaging her engine. The engine
was successfully raised in 1886.
(Thunder Bay Historical Society Collection)

Full particulars of how she got on there are not known yet. We have had very thick smoky weather here lately. She is laying in about 4 feet of water on her starboard side and about five hundred yards from the Little Schooner Island Rocks. She is listed astarboard and full of water. She is surrounded with very shole water. The foggy weather on the ninth prevented us from seeing the main shore."

August 12: "Wrecking party are at work raising the machinery of tug George Hand."

Thus the *Algoma* stranding resulted in the wreck of wrecking tug *George Hand*. The George Hand had been built in 1868 at Buffalo. She was purchased in 1884 by Calvin Curry and Albert Gilbert, who operated her out of Algonac, Michigan. At the time of loss she was chartered to the salvage firm of Merriman & Fowler.

Loss of the *George Hand* apparently did not hamper salvage efforts on the *Algoma*, for on August 26 the schooner *L. L. Lamb* arrived in Owen Sound with the *Algoma's* engine and reported the boilers had been raised and set ashore for her return. Eventually, the boilers and numerous other small engines and appartus were brought into Owen Sound on the *Lamb*. The engine and boilers were reused in the *Manitoba*, built by Polson Iron Works of Owen Sound in 1889 for the Canadian Pacific Railway as the *Algoma's* replacement.

The wreck of the *Algoma* resulted in the largest loss of life of any Isle Royale shipwreck with at least 37 persons missing. Because the ship's purser was among those lost, an accurate number will probably never be known. One can only imagine the magnitude of tradegy if the *Algoma* had been lost on her first trip up the lake with 1,100 passengers aboard.

The *Algoma* accident still poses one of Isle Royale's intriguing shipwreck questions. Where is the missing bow, fully two-thirds of this once-magnificent passenger steamer? And further, the remains of the *George Hand* have not been reported since Keeper Malone made his August 12, 1886, journal entry. Perhaps some day these two of Isle Royale's "missing" vessels will be found and further documented.

PASSAGE ISLAND LIGHTHOUSE (1882)

As early as 1871 the U.S. Lighthouse Board requested an appropriation for establishing a lighthouse on Passage Island: "This discovery of the silver mines on Lake Superior (primarily Silver Islet north of Isle Royale), and consequent sudden and remarkable increase of travel and traffic to that region, render it desirable that a lighthouse should be built on Passage Island, to mark the channel between it and Isle Royale. This island is difficult of access, and therefore any structure put there will cost more than if erected at some more accessible point. There is recommended an appropriation of $18,000 for the purpose indicated."

After repeated requests, an $18,000 conditional appropriation was made in 1875. The condition was that the Dominion of Canada had to build a lighthouse "on Colchester Reef, to the eastward of the mouth of the Detroit River" on Lake Erie. It was a simple exchange of international courtesy designed to safeguard vessels of both countries.

However, this condition delayed plans to build Passage Island Light for five years as the Canadian government worked out appropriations and plans for Colchester Reef Light. By 1880 Canada had made sufficient progress toward establishing the Colchester Reef Light so that actual construction could begin at Passage Island while similar work went forward on the Stannard Rock and Sand Island lights, also on Lake Superior. These three projects kept the lighthouse supply vessel *Warrington* constantly on the move, shuttling men, equipment, materials and supplies.

The keystone on the keeper's dwelling was set in 1881, and Passage Island Light was completed in 1882, with the lamp first illuminated on the night of July 1, just three days before Stannard Rock's. (It was to be three years before the Colchester Reef Light was completed.) The station was originally equipped with a fog bell, but in 1882 installation of a steam fog signal was completed "in duplicate." In that first season the signal was used 174 hours. More than 20 years later, in the 1906 season, the signal saw a record of 902 hours of use, consuming 50 tons of coal brought up the steep bluff on a narrow tramway.

When first established in 1882, Passage Island Light was a fixed red light illuminated by a 4th Order* oil-burning wick lamp. In 1897 this was changed to a flashing white lamp, greatly increasing its visibility. In 1913 the light's intensity was increased nearly tenfold, to 50,000 candlepower, with conversion from the old wick lamp to a new incandescent oil-vapor lamp using a mantle. The light was electrified in 1928. The station is now automated and unmanned.

While Silver Islet's rich silver mine (the original reason for constructing Passage Island Light) soon became idle, the growing Canadian Lakehead grain trade made Passage Island Light one of the most important on Lake Superior. Its importance has not diminished after a century of service.

Passage Island lighthouse and adjacent steam generating building being inspected by visitors from Isle Royale, as seen in an old postcard view. (C. Patrick Labadie Collection)

The handsome passenger steamer **<u>MONARCH</u>** in the
1890s on a trip to Duluth Harbor.
(**Minnesota Historical Society Collection**)

MONARCH (1890-1906)

For fully two dozen years Passage Island Light served mariners traversing the lake near Isle Royale's northeastern tip with the loss of only the *Algoma* in 1885 and that several miles away. This enviable record was shattered on a snowy December 6, 1906, when the handsome steamer *Monarch* crashed blindly into the Palisades of Blake Point while trying to get a fix on either the light or fog signal on Passage Island.

The passenger-package freighter *Monarch* had been built in 1890 at Sarnia, Ontario, for the Beatty brothers and their Northern Navigation Company. Captain Edward Robertson was selected as *Monarch's* first, and only, master. He was superbly qualified with nearly twenty years of Great Lakes sailing.

Monarch's graceful hull was timbered and planked with carefully selected white oak. Supporting truss arches along her sides were nearly invisible when skillfully incorporated into her design. Her cabins were finely finished of the best materials by craftsmen both skilled and dedicated. Her cost was a now-modest $150,000. She stretched a little over 240 feet with a 900-horsepower, triple-expansion steam engine.

The *Monarch* was making her last run of the season when lost. She had offloaded general cargo in Port Arthur after a rough trip up the lake, and she immediately took on a load of bagged grain and flour and a variety of general cargo including canned salmon, red lead paint, and several cases of beer bottles filled with grain samples. She also welcomed aboard a sparse 12 passengers bound for Sarnia.

At 5:20 p.m. on December 6, *Monarch* cleared Port Arthur downbound. She rounded Thunder Cape, at the foot of the Sleeping Giant, about an hour and 20 minutes later, setting her regular course for Passage Island in a "fair breeze from the norwest" and amidst "very heavy steam rising from the water with snow at times."

Captain Robertson later described the rest of the voyage: "We continued on this course for the full time to the Passage Island, that is two hours and twenty minutes. We put the (taffrail) log out at Thunder Cape in the usual way. We caught a glimpse of the Passage Island Light twice. When we had run about the full time for the Passage as above mentioned, the Second Mate was sent back to examine the log, and he found the same frozen up, and that it had only registered ten miles. When we had run our full time for the Passage, we hauled down on a course S.E. by E. ¼ E., being the regular course for Whitefish Point. We continued on this course for six minutes and then hauled her back E. by S. ¾ S. to allow for leeway. The weather at this time was dense with snow and fog from the water, and we could not see anything. In a very few minutes we struck..."

There were 32 crewmen aboard, in addition to the 12 passengers, including Captain Robertson and the only woman, Miss Rachel McCormick, who was both "lady's maid" and assistant cook. Each was tossed about in the impact, but no one was injured. *Monarch's* stern settled quickly and she took a strong list to port, but the crew was able to launch one lifeboat. After a vain attempt to reach shore, they returned to the ship.

A new scheme was worked out. A long rope was tied to a wooden ladder which was then lowered over the bow. John D. "Jack" McCallum, younger brother of the *Monarch's* second mate, who was working his passage to Sarnia as a deckhand, volunteered to descend the ladder.

Rope, ladder, and young McCallum were than swung pendulum-fashion until he was finally close enough to leap ashore. McCallum carefully worked his way up the ice-covered rock bluff to the ridgetop and used his lifeline to pull a length of sturdy rope up from the ship below. He secured this hawser to a tree. Then, one by one, hand over hand, the entire group, save one crewman who had earlier fallen overboard, went ashore leaving only Captain Robertson. He stubbornly refused to leave his ship and spent that first night aboard. The following day he was persuaded to come ashore.

For two days and three nights the crew did their best to keep warm and dry with little nourishment. On the third day, December 9, a small boat approached from Passage Island bringing the assistant keeper, who was investigating the signal fires. He and the ship's purser set out to flag down the next freighter and get word back to Port Arthur. Later in the day, they did stop the steamer *Edmonton*, which returned with the message. Early the next morning, tugs *James Whalen* and *Laura Grace* set out for the wreck scene with doctors, medicine and supplies, rescuing the survivors on December 10 and returning them to Port Arthur.

More than a week later, the *Monarch's* crew completed their downbound journey to Sarnia where one newspaper reported, "Pandemonium broke loose when the steamer *Huronic* arrived...with the survivors of the wrecked steamer *Monarch* on board. It appeared as if the entire town came down to the wharf to welcome the shipwrecked crew. A brass band added to the din of whistles... Every man was a hero, but it remained for the woman, Miss Rachel McCormick, one of the crew, to carry off the real honors." She had withstood the elements best of all the crew. Even Captain Robertson commented that she was "the best man among them." In 1907 John D. McCallum was awarded the Board of Trade's Royal Humane Society Medal for his courageous part in the rescue.

Monarch's wreck was purchased in September 1908 from the underwriters by Reid Wrecking Company of Sarnia and Port Huron. About 25 days, 14 men, two barges, a tug, and two divers were invested in salvage efforts. Captain Reid commented, "We took everything of value out of the wreck, having found conditions such that we were able to make a very complete job of it. We have the boilers, engines, dynamos, chains, windlasses, etc. loaded on the barge ready to be taken to Sarnia." But much was lost when when their scow *Bennington* sank on Lake Superior October 5, 1908. *Monarch's* engine survived but was not reused.

The *Monarch's* hull is now badly broken, partly from the salvage operation and partly from ice since portions of the hull are in relatively shallow water.

Wreck of the <u>MONARCH</u>, as viewed in
mid-December 1906. She is broken in two,
amidships, with the stern submerged.
(Thunder Bay Historical Society Collection)

BLAKE POINT
LIGHT (1917)

What is often called "the end of Isle Royale," more properly known as Blake Point, is the site of the island's smallest and newest lighthouse structure. It is a simple, steel skeleton tower somewhat reminiscent of a windmill. It was first lighted on October 27, 1917, nearly 11 years after the *Monarch's* loss. Its original mission was to replace a gas and bell buoy which marked the easterly edge of an 18-foot shoal just off the point. Later a sector light was added to cover from 270° to 285°, the area around Canoe Rocks to the west of the point. The 100 candle-power light is battery operated and shown at a height of 20 feet above land and 40 feet above the lake, visible about 10 to 12 miles on a clear night. Diamond-shaped targets on the tower serve as day markers.

Blake Point Light marks the icy tip of Isle Royale and safe passage around dreaded Canoe Rocks to the west.

(Author's Collection)

CHESTER A. CONGDON (1907-1918)

"We were running under slow speed, at about nine miles per hour, and I figured on stopping on account of the fog until we could locate something. Then at eight minutes after one in the afternoon, she fetched up–rounded." That's how Captain Charles J. Autterson described the last few minutes aboard the *Chester A. Congdon* on November 6, 1918, as she ran up on the southwestern edge of the shoal off Canoe Rocks, west of Blake Point.

Just the day before, the *Congdon* had loaded 390,154 bushels of wheat at Fort William. Captain Autterson maneuvered the *Congdon* away from the dock at 2:28 a.m. on November 6, proceeded out into Thunder Bay and moved along briskly until just outside Thunder Cape. There he was greeted by heavy seas driven by gale winds from the southwest. After running just seven or eight miles, he brought the *Congdon* about and returned to restless shelter behind the Cape.

After several hours the winds began to diminish, and at 10 a.m. Captain Autterson decided that the worst was over. He got underway 15 minutes later and passed Thunder Cape again at 10:40 for Passage Island. There was still some sea running and thick fog drifted over the lake. The plan was to run for about two and a half hours, then come to anchor if they could not get a fix on either Passage Island Light or fog signal. The time had nearly expired when she struck.

Chester A. Congdon of Duluth in 1912
(Northeast Minnesota Historical Center Collection)

Captain Charles W. Autterson is
shown here with derby and flower in his
lapel as he posed with other Great Lakes ship masters
after speaking on the need for improved
lighthouses and other aids to navigation before
Congress in 1912.
(Donald Zeh Collection)

**On a blustery day, the bulk freighter
CHESTER A. CONGDON enters Duluth Harbor for
cargo of grain.
(K.E. Thro Collection)**

**Wreck of the 532 ft. CHESTER A. CONGDON,
largest vessel lost in Isle Royale waters.
(Canal Park Marine Museum Collection)**

18

Captain Autterson said, "We immediately lowered boats and sent one boat over to Passage Island, about 7 miles away, to try and secure some assistance from the lighthouse keeper, if possible. Then, the second Mate took another boat, a fisherman's launch, from Canoe Rocks in to Port William. He had two fishermen with him. The launch became disabled, and they did not reach Fort William until six o'clock Thursday morning (November 7)."

Meanwhile, the *Congdon* rested on the reef. Although there were more people aboard the ship than usual, 37, including Captain Autterson and four naval reservists assigned there during the war, there were no lives lost and no major injuries reported.

Second Mate Schwab and the two anonymous Isle Royale fishermen brought word of the wreck to Fort William where the Canadian Towing and Wrecking Company immediately sent out tug *A.B. Conmee* with wrecking barge *Empire.* They were joined later by tug *Sarnia.* The salvagers managed to take off 30,000 bushels of wheat before a vicious 55-mile per hour gale on November 8 forced them into shelter behind Blake Point. When able to return to the wreck on November 10, they found the *Congdon* badly broken with her stern submerged. Scarcely 10,000 more bushels of wheat were salvaged before the ship and cargo were declared a total loss by the insurance company.

Later that winter the *Chester A. Congdon* was purchased by James Playfair of Midland, Ontario, for $10,000. Plans were made to return to the wreck site in the spring and begin salvage since the bow and stern sections remained attached with the bow still above water. However, in the spring of 1919, salvagers found only Lake Superior's icy waves lightly massaging Canoe Rock's baldness. Below, lay the once handsome freighter, broken in two, well beyond economical recovery. Thus the *Chester A. Congdon* became the largest vessel lost on all the Great Lakes up to that time, as well as becoming the lakes' first million dollar loss, all without loss of life. She remains the largest vessel lost in Isle Royale waters.

The *Chester A. Congdon* had been built in 1907 at South Chicago as the bulk freighter *Salt Lake City.* She was renamed for a prominent Duluth lawyer and financier who had strong financial ties to mining and grain interests. The *Congdon* was 532 feet long and powered by a 1,765 horsepower, triple-expansion steam engine. Exploring this wreck is a two-dive operation because the bow and stern are on opposite sides of Congdon Shoal.

EMPEROR (1910-1947)

It was only through lucky coincidence that the U.S. Coast Guard Cutter *Kimball* was within minutes of the Canadian ore freighter *Emperor* when she struck a shoal extending northeasterly from the dreaded Canoe Rocks, just west of Blake Point. "It was too bad, but I'm glad we were there to do what we could," said Lt. Calvin R. Clark, master of the *Kimball*. The *Emperor's* urgent distress call was received at 4:10 a.m. on board the *Kimball*, which was lying at anchor for the night in Tobin Harbor, where she had been working on aids to navigation. The *Kimball* was underway in seven minutes and picked up the first survivors only half an hour later.

Lt. Clark said, "We launched a motorboat from the *Kimball* and picked up four survivors from an overturned boat. Then we picked up seven on Canoe Rocks, and ten from another lifeboat half-filled with water. It looked as though the crew did not have time to launch a boat properly." Twenty-one persons were rescued and the body of the first cook recovered in the *Kimball's* initial rescue efforts. All were transported to Port Arthur. Additional search later in the day recovered a second woman's body, the porter. Ten remained missing, some trapped within the ship.

Canada Steamship Lines, Ltd., owner of the *Emperor*, chartered the *Coastal Queen* out of Port Arthur to continue searching the area. They also enlisted hardhat diver E.J. "Doc" Fowler of Port Arthur to search for additional remains while exploring the

possiblity of salvage. After several fruitless days, the insurance company declared the *Emperor* a total loss, beyond recovery, and the ten missing crewmen presumed dead and buried at sea. The remains of at least two of the missing were located years later, one in the engine room and one in the boiler room.

The precise events leading up to the wreck of the *Emperor* in the early morning darkness of June 4, 1947, are clouded even in the official report of investigation. Part of the problem in pinpointing the cause of the stranding and foundering is that the two men who might have given the clearest testimony were lost, First Mate James Morey and Wheelsman John Prokup, both on duty at the time of the accident.

Principal blame for the loss was placed by the Court of Investigation on the first mate for not keeping a "proper watch." However, this was qualified by the Court, saying "that the system which prevailed, which required the First Mate to be in charge of the loading of the ship during the period when he should have been off duty, resulted in his becoming overtired, suffering as he was from loss of sleep." Thus the *Emperor* was beaten as much by the system as she was by the reef which broke her back. Today's lake sailors stand two four-hour watches, with four hours on duty, eight off, four on, and eight off, to prevent the fatigue and subsequent carelessness or inattention to duty which plagued the *Emperor's* first mate.

Ordinarily, a vessel clearing Thunder Bay would steer a course of 138° true from the Welcome Islands, inside the bay, until abreast of Thunder Cape Light where a

When launched in 1910 the 525 ft steamer <u>EMPEROR</u> was the largest ship ever built in Canada.
(Author's Collection)

<u>COASTAL QUEEN</u>, out of Port Arthur, used the forward mast of the <u>EMPORER</u> as a mooring while hardhat diver E.J. "Doc" Fowler searched below for the lost.
(E.J. "Doc" Fowler Collection)

<u>EMPEROR's</u> pilothouse submerged, but clearly visible, soon after the wreck in 1947.
(E.J. "Doc" Fowler Collection)

course change to 098° true would be effected. The Court determined, however, that the *Emperor* probably did not make the course change opposite Thunder Cape Light, but three miles beyond when opposite Trowbridge Island. This brought the *Emperor* onto a collision course with the northeasterly shoal off Canoe Rocks. The *Emperor* struck head-on, at full speed, and without warning to any of her 33-man crew.

Second Mate Peter Craven was in his bunk when the *Emperor* struck. He recalled, "I felt the crash and leaped out of bed. I grabbed my clothes, seized a life belt, and ran to the crew's quarters to awaken those who were still asleep. I got the men on deck and Captain Walkinshaw told them stand by. I knew it was only a matter of time before she'd go under. When I got back on deck, the *Emperor* was listing sharply and that's when the captain gave the abandon ship signal. The first lifeboat was lowered and floated without too much trouble. Some of the men went over the side on ropes. Others jumped. I jumped in later and managed to get into the second lifeboat. After being thrown from the lifeboat, I came to the surface and managed to cling to the bottom side. Three others did likewise. We waited like that until the U.S. Coast Guard Cutter *Kimball* rescued us."

"It was pitch black," recalled Wheelsman William Randall, "and I couldn't see a thing after we struck, but I knew something serious had happened. What happened? I don't know. I guess the captain and the men in the wheelhouse are the only ones who could give the real dope and they are missing."

When it was completed in 1910, the *Emperor* was the largest vessel built in Canada, stretching to 525 feet overall. A powerful 2,200-horsepower, triple-expansion steam engine gave her a speed of 13 miles per hour while carrying a full cargo. She was carrying 10,429 tons of natural iron ore, near maximum capacity, when lost. Today there are many visible signs still on the wreck of those last agonizing moments, torn and twisted hull plating, collapsed interior bulkheads. However badly broken the vessel remains an *"Emperor"* of the Lakes.

ISLE ROYALE LIGHTHOUSE (1875)

Early in the 1870s, vessel men operating in conjunction with copper mining and commercial fishing interests urged the U.S. Lighthouse Board to establish a light marking safe passage to the large 295 ft Island Mine wharf in Siskiwit Bay. Congress responded favorably on March 3, 1873. The initial survey work was completed in 1874, selecting Menagerie Island as the most suitable location, about midway along Isle Royale's south side and at the entry to Siskiwit Bay. Undoubtedly the site was selected also with the idea of eventually phasing out the Rock Harbor Light.

Work finally began in 1875 with labor from several mainland communities. A feverish pace was set so the structure could be completed by early fall when lake storms become more frequent and more severe. The fixed white light burned for the first time on the evening of September 20, 1875, atop a 55-foot octagonal, whitewashed sandstone tower connected to the adjacent keeper's dwelling by a covered passageway of unpainted reddish brown sandstone. Most of the stone was probably quarried near Jacobsville on the Keweenaw Peninsula, but some is also reported to have been cut even more locally. Huge iron shutters were installed to protect window areas in severe storms when waves crash right over the low, rocky island.

There have been many changes to the lighthouse site since it began operation. A boathouse, a landing crib, boatways and a four-ton, boat-hoisting winch were installed in 1891. Five years later the boat landing was lengthened 16 feet to accommodate larger lighthouse tenders. The boatways were also extended by 38 feet and the crib rebuilt. In 1906 a concrete block oilhouse was added to store 500 gallons of fuel for the oil-wick lamp and heating.

Perhaps the most significant change came in 1939 when the Coast Guard took over responsibility for the Isle Royale Light and determined that there was insufficient vessel traffic in the area to warrant the expense of maintaining a keeper. The light was not abandoned, but automated by conversion to a battery-powered lamp. Since then the automatic equipment has been updated several times, and by 1985, plans were being made to convert the light to solar power. The 4th Order, flashing white light is visible about 16 miles and is frequently comforting to mariners who choose a more northerly route than customary, sailing in the lee of Isle Royale in order to avoid heavy weather in the open lake.

The best remembered of lighthouse keepers anywhere around Isle Royale was John H. Malone, second keeper of the Isle Royale Light. In the more than two decades that Malone was keeper, he raised a very large family, and one son, John A., succeeded his father as keeper. With nearly a dozen mouths to feed, the family relied on fishing, real rock gardening, raising cows and hunting seagull eggs as more than pastimes. Malone also managed to get into tourism using the 44-foot schooner *Northern Belle* to take out parties of excursionists.

Isle Royale Lighthouse on Menagerie Island was
home for the large family of Keeper John H. Malone.
This photo was taken in 1911.

(Janet Leibel Collection)

GLENLYON (1893-1924)

Just northeast of Menagerie Island and the Isle Royale Lighthouse is a reef which was nameless until after November 1, 1924. It was then, on this reef that ever since has borne her name, that the *Glenlyon* of the Great Lakes Transportation Company fleet of Midland, Ontario, impaled herself while seeking safe anchorage in the sheltered waters of Siskiwit Bay.

The *Glenlyon* had completed 31 seasons on the lakes which saw her laden with iron ore, coal, and grain, as well as package freight. Built in 1893 as the *William H. Gratwick*, she entered American registry as a 328-foot bulk carrier. In 1912 her name was changed to *Minnekahta* and she shifted to carrying package freight and a few passengers. Retaining her name, she crossed over to Canadian registry in 1914. Her name was later changed to *Glenlyon* and she returned to bulk trades carrying primarily grain for her new owner.

Downbound from Fort William to Port Colborne, Ontario, on October 30, 1924, the *Glenlyon* encountered a stormy Lake Superior just outside Thunder Cape. Captain William Taylor brought his ship about and returned to safe anchorage off the Welcome Islands in Thunder Bay. The storm quieted down the following night and the *Glenlyon's* anchors were shipped to begin her voyage once more.

Shortly before midnight the *Glenlyon* cleared Passage Island Light at the northern end of Isle Royale, only to be met again by an angry, storm-tossed lake. In the face of

40-mile per hour winds and rising eight-foot seas, Captain Taylor sought safe anchorage again.

In the early morning hours of November 1, the *Glenlyon's* crew caught glimpse of the Isle Royale Light. Calmer waters lay just beyond Menagerie Island. As the *Glenlyon* made the starboard turn into Siskiwit Bay, she rolled and pitched, lifting her propeller partly out of the water, sending vibrations throughout the ship. She responded sluggishly to her rudder. Then, without warning, the *Glenlyon* scraped over a reef, quickly stopping as the moan of steel tearing from steel reverberated over her full length. The *Glenlyon* was soon dead in the water as her engine room flooded. Her back was broken.

Wireless operator Roger Paige was thrown from his chair on the initial impact. Recovering quickly, he tapped out a distress signal as Captain Taylor ordered every man to his post. The government wireless station in Port Arthur received the urgent message, and by six a.m. the tug *Strathmore* had been ordered to the scene. Two steamers, the *Glenlinnie* and *Glensannox*, also picked up the distress signal. They altered course for the stricken ship but were forced by the weather to stand off about a half mile at first. By 2 p.m. the *Glenlinnie* had maneuvered alongside the *Glenlyon* and was able to begin taking off the crew. They were quickly transferred to the *Glensannox*, which had positioned herself to act as a floating breakwall for the other two ships.

Steamer <u>GLENLYON</u>, as seen about 1920,
passing through the Soo Locks.
(Herman G. Runge Collection, Milwaukee Public Library)

Eagle Harbor, Michigan, Coast Guardsmen had also picked up the *Glenlyon's* signal, but had difficulty with their boat and passed the word on to the crew at the Portage Lake Ship Canal (Keweenaw Peninsula). The canal crew reached the ship about midnight. Once on the scene, they began searching for Mate McLaughlin and Watchman Roy. They had become separated from the wreck in a lifeboat while they were examining the ship for exterior hull damage. The two men drifted for 23 hours until Coast Guardsmen found them near the head of Siskiwit Bay and transferred them to the *Glenconna*, which had also stopped by to render assistance. The *Glenlyon's* crew survived intact, although a few suffered from exposure and minor injuries.

During the next few days, salvage crews lightered 10,000 bushels of wheat from the *Glenlyon's* hold. The *Glenlyon* clung fast to the reef throughout the winter of 1924-25. But as spring storms came, she rotated and shifted off the reef. She slipped beneath the surface by the end of April 1925, taking all hope of salvage with her. Exploring the wreck now, scuba divers report the *Glenlyon's* anchors still in place in their respective pockets. They speculate that the *Glenlyon* might have been saved if salvagers had dropped her anchors in an attempt to hold her steady over the winter. This had been done successfully in 1903-04 when salvage crews had to abandon the *John T. Hutchinson* over the winter off Eagle Harbor.

KAMLOOPS (1924-1927)

Isle Royale's major shipwrecks still hold many secrets deep within themselves even though they have been rather thoroughly explored and photographed by sport divers and professional underwater archeologists. The Canadian package freighter *Kamloops*, lost on the island's north side in 1927, still holds many secrets. She kept one important one for nearly 50 years -- her location.

The *Kamloops* was upbound at the Soo Locks on December 4, 1927, headed for Thunder Bay. After learning of the severe storm then engulfing eastern Lake Superior, Captain William Brian decided that he would anchor in Whitefish Bay with the many other ships already sheltered there.

This was to be the last upbound trip of the season for the *Kamloops*. She was a 250-foot, or Welland Canal-size, package freighter built in 1924 at Sunderland, England, for Canada Steamship Lines and service on the Great Lakes. A sister ship was launched only two weeks later. This was the *Lethbridge* and she remained active until the 1959 opening of the St. Lawrence Seaway with its new and larger locks, which permitted longer, more economical vessels to enter the trade. She was finally sold for scrap early in the 1960s, but her longevity indicates the integrity of the *Kamloops*, built in the same yard of identical design and materials.

On her last voyage the *Kamloops* carried the mixed freight she was accustomed to. Her most valuable cargo was new papermaking machinery for the mill at Port Arthur. Her cargo also included imported teas and candies, toothpaste, high-top men's shoes, and new life preservers for a boat undergoing a name change at the Port Arthur shipyard, as well as a large consignment of building materials such as rolled fence wire and matching gates, tar paper, and hundreds of bundles of water pipe in various sizes. On her return voyage to Montreal, the *Kamloops* would have carried either bulk grain or package freight.

It was December 6 before the storm appeared to break and vessels that had anchored in Whitefish Bay began moving again. Three vessels set out, one behind the other: first the *Quedoc*, followed by the *Winnipeg*, and then the *Kamloops*. They were within sight of one another during the remaining daylight hours. As night fell the storm again erupted, coming first out the northeast, shifting to the northwest in the 24 hours that followed. Now the vessels only occasionally saw each other's lights; none carried wireless, but whistle signals were exchanged now and then.

Early that evening, December 6, the *Quedoc's* watchman spotted massive rocks ahead, quickly maneuvered, and blew a danger signal which was answered by the following *Winnipeg*. The *Winnipeg* signaled the *Kamloops* but received no response. Visibility was poor and the light from Passage Island was blocked. Later, the *Winnipeg's* captain got a glimpse of the *Kamloops* still plodding along, but heavily laden with ice, particularly on deck, where she carried much of the building material.

Welland Canaller **KAMLOOPS** as seen soon after
arrival in Montreal from England
where she was built for the Lakes.
(University of Detroit Marine Collection)

The *Quedoc* made it into Thunder Bay, quickly loaded grain, and departed. Meanwhile, Captain Kenneth LaRush sheltered the *Winnipeg* for a day among the numerous islands on the Canadian coast. This was not an uncommon occurrence so late in the season, and without wireless there was little concern in port for vessels a day or two late. However, upon reaching port, Captain LaRush pleaded in vain with the company's local representatives to let him go back out and search for the *Kamloops*. He was so incensed by this apparent indifference that he promptly quit, sailing for many seasons thereafter for the rival N.M. Paterson fleet.

No real search for the *Kamloops* began until she was more than a week overdue. Ten days of extensive search along most of the eastern Lake Superior shoreline on both the American and Canadian sides failed to turn up a single clue. The *Kamloops* had vanished, although her owners speculated that she may have sheltered as did the *Winnipeg* and simply become frozen in.

The *Kamloops'* fate was not known until the following spring when the bodies of nine crew members were found near Todd Harbor and Twelve O'Clock Point, along with several hatch covers, the pilot house roof, assorted life preservers, portions of cargo, and the badly broken remains of one lifeboat. The *Kamloops* was still missing, but apparently had foundered nearby. Canada Steamship Lines spokesmen insisted that all 21 of the crew perished quickly and that no one could have been saved by a more prompt or thorough search.

However, at least two of the crew had made it ashore alive, First Mate Henry Genest and Assistant Steward Alice Bettridge. Genest's body was located last, more than 300 feet onshore. Miss Bettridge was by her own account the last survivor. In a note cast adrift in a bottle she wrote, "I am the last one alive, freezing and starving on Isle Royale. I just want Mom and Dad to know my fate." The note was not found until nearly a year after the wreck. The signature and handwriting were later verified by Miss Bettridge's parents.

Over the first winter, the Bettridges, like so many other crewmen's families, had sought solace where they could. They invited a local medium to attempt to intercede. The medium came to their house in Southampton, Ontario, and asked for the family Bible and the key to their front door. She inserted the key in the Bible, and the book opened to a passage which the medium read silently. In a few moments she said that Alice's body would be found on a large island. Alice Bettridge's remains were located in the spring of 1928 and returned for burial in the Southampton Cemetery.

Still, the *Kamloops* was missing. Although many divers searched, she was not located for nearly 50 years. In 1977 sport divers found the *Kamloops* about 300 feet offshore with the stern in the shallowest water, about 175 feet deep and nearest shore, and with the bow more than 250 feet deep. Curiously, the *Kamloops* rests almost directly on her starboard side. There is no apparent evidence of any damage to the hull or steering apparatus. Significant, though, is

Above, the **KAMLOOPS**, as she appeared when lost, with reddish hull, white cabins and bulwarks, and buff colored booms for handling package freight.
(Public Archives of Canada)

At right is the first photograph of the **KAMLOOPS** after discovery in 1977.
(Ken Engelbrecht Photograph)

her missing smokestack and railing damage on the port-side boat deck, that is, on the high side of the wreck as it rests on the bottom.

One theory on the *Kamloops'* loss suggests that, heavily laden with ice, she lost her smokestack over the port side as she was making the starboard turn off Thunder Cape toward Port Arthur, and within five to ten minutes became a steamer without steam. The stack's breaking away would have damaged a large steam line running from the top of the boilers to the main whistle, as well as preventing the boilers from being properly fired.

From that point on the vessel would simply have drifted before the northerly winds. Captain Brian probably prepared about half the crew, those least necessary to handle the ship, to abandon ship under direction of First Mate Genest. Sighting Isle Royale's coastline in the blackness, or perhaps hearing the surf crashing against her icy shore, he probably ordered the lifeboat launched. It may have capsized offshore, dumping its human cargo into the freezing waters.

The *Kamloops*, powerless and carrying a heavy list due to the tons of ice on her deck, capsized and plunged to the bottom, spilling off her deck cargo. The engine telegraph in the engine room shows "Finished with Engines" as ordered from the wheelhouse and answered by the Chief Engineer. There would have been no time and no reason to do this if the engine had not already been rendered useless well in advance of the *Kamloops'* foundering.

ROCK OF AGES LIGHTHOUSE (1908)

The southwestern end of Isle Royale is somewhat less rugged than the northeastern end, and today vessel traffic passing Rock of Ages some five miles offshore is considerably less than that off Passage Island. This was not always true. For more than three-quarters of a century, there was regularly scheduled waterborne commerce between the Canadian Lakehead at Fort William and Port Arthur and the American Lakehead at Duluth and Superior. Vessel traffic along the Minnesota shore needed the guidance of a powerful beacon. In addition to the vessels which regularly traded between the Lakeheads, there were vessels that frequented the area to avoid weather farther out on the lake.

The initial request for the construction of Rock of Ages Lighthouse in 1895 said, "During the season of southerly and westerly winds, many vessels bound to and from Duluth, by taking a course along the north shore of the lake and in lee of Isle Royale, are enabled to run when the lake is too rough for the more southerly course. A light and fog-signal on the dangerous rocks off the westerly end of Isle Royale would be a valuable aid to these vessels. It is therefore proposed to establish a light and fog-signal station on the Rock of Ages. . ." The request was further supported by the 1877 loss of the sidewheel steamer *Cumberland* on nearby Rock of Ages Reef.

ock of Ages Lighthouse begins to take shape.
Workmen lived at the Washington Club in Washington
arbor in the early stages of construction.
(Author's Collection)

ower formed more quickly once workmen
gan living "on the Rock."
(Author's Collection)

The Lighthouse was originally black and buff
colored, but now is black and white.
(Author's Collection)

The 1895 request for $50,000 was repeated verbatim for five years, but by 1900, estimated construction costs had escalated to $125,000, and there had been another shipwreck, the *Henry Chisholm*, in 1898 on Rock of Ages Reef. Still, there was no congressional action. Finally, ten years after the process began, the Lighthouse Board reduced the initial site survey and planning request to $25,000 which was granted in 1905. The following year an additional $50,000 was approved, with the final $50,000 installment coming in 1907.

Actual work began in 1907 with crews blasting and reshaping Rock of Ages to accept the steel cylindrical base some 30 feet high and 50 feet in diameter. Workmen lived first at the Washington Club in Washington Harbor, later moving to the "Rock" itself. The structural portion of the base and tower were completed in this one season including reinforced concrete floors, all tile partitions and all interior trim and plastering, as well as the erection of the watch room and lantern, the installation of the illuminating and fog-signal apparatus, and the water-supply and steam-heating systems."

Rock of Ages Light, a temporary, 3rd order* fixed red light, was illuminated on October 22, 1908, atop the 10-story structure. The permanent lamp and lens were ordered in 1909 from Paris after an additional appropriation for this purpose was approved. This Fresnel lens with incandescent oil-vapor lamp was the first of its kind installed on the Great Lakes. The new lamp was a 2nd Order* white light showing a double flash every 10 seconds. The new

"lightning light" was first shown on September 15, 1910.

From a distance, Rock of Ages Light, with its white tower and black base and lantern, looks like a spark plug. Originally, the entire structure, except the lantern, was painted a less-distinctive buff color.

Tower entry is made at the engine or generator room level. Below are the cellar, where the heating plant is located, and the sub-cellar, used for storage. Above the entry level is the office; the kitchen and mess room are on the next level, topped by the keeper and first assistant's quarters. Above are quarters for the second and third assistants. Still higher is the watch room from which it is often possible to see over low-hanging fog, just as it was on the day in May 1933 when Keeper John F. Soldenski saw the passenger steamer *George M. Cox* racing for Rock of Ages Reef. At the very top is the lantern room where the lens system has its focal plane 117 feet, 1 and 3/8 inches above the lake.

Rock of Ages Light, frequently visible for more than 20 miles, still serves as the primary beacon above northwestern Lake Superior. The light was automated in 1977, and by 1985 plans were completed to upgrade the equipment by conversion to solar power. The sun-powered light, with its collector panels and bank of rechargeable batteries, is expected to reduce considerably operating and maintenance costs. The magnificent 2nd Order* Fresnel lens has been removed and preserved for public display.

CUMBERLAND (1871-1877)

More than a hundred years ago, the Candian passenger and package freight side-wheeler *Cumberland* came to rest atop Rock of Ages Reef a mile southwest of the present Rock of Ages Lighthouse. The *Cumberland*, with glistening white wooden hull and cabins, was a handsome craft with her huge paddle wheels churning into the lake. She was built at a cost of $101,000 in 1871 at Port Robinson, Ontario, to sail the Lake Superior Navigation Company's Collingwood (Georgian Bay) and Lake Superior run.

Though small by today's standards, the *Cumberland* compared favorably in length with her contemporaries at 204 feet. She was powered by a one-cylinder, walking-beam steam engine removed from another, older sidewheeler, *Columbian*, built in 1846. Switching engines was a relatively common practice then and is still done today, although now the entire engine room compartment is incorporated into the newer vessel.

The *Cumberland* completed her sea trials in October 1871, too late to enter service that season. In May 1872 she began running between Collingwood and Fort William, sometimes adding a trip to Duluth. She was described in 1872 as "fitted up in the most elegant style" and ready to " meet the highest expectations of the traveling public," which included businessmen, a handful of tourists and scores of immigrants seeking work and a new life in the wild Lake Superior country.

Considering the era of her operation, the *Cumberland* had no more than the usual number of scrapes, near-misses, groundings and other excitement in her six-year history. Only a few days before stranding at Isle Royale, she was caught in an unusual July snow squall and ran aground near Silver Isle just north of Isle Royale. She limped into Port Arthur four days later to make temporary repairs and again set out, this time for Duluth. It was on this journey that she ran up on Rock of Ages Reef on July 24, 1877, despite clear weather and only a modest breeze. She must have been making good speed at the time since she was reported to have "run on so hard that all the forward half of the vessel is on the reef."

Apparently the shoal area where the *Cumberland* stranded was "not laid down on the Candian charts" then in use. Rumors spread quickly that Captain James Parsons and his vessel were "led into the scrape by relying on charts of Lake Superior furnished by the United States" although this allegation proved totally unfounded; U.S. charts clearly showed only "six feet of water and rock bottom at the point where the vessel struck." It was a faulty Canadian chart which apparently resulted in the accident although Parsons had been safely over this route dozens of times before. What caused him to venture so near Rock of Ages on this voyage may never be known.

Despite the efforts of several tugs and steamers to release her, the *Cumberland* remained steadfast on the reef. Finally on

August 6, amidst unusually foul weather, she was abandoned. By mid-August the *Cumberland* was reported broken in two and rapidly disintegrating. Her registry was closed 18 days later.

Early in September came this report, "The steamer *Cumberland*. . .has gotten tired of being hoisted on the reef on which she has been for some time, and has gone to rest. She is now quietly lying on the bed of Lake Superior. Some wreckers went to look for her lately, but could not find her." The *Cumberland* was valued at about $48,000 when lost although she was insured for only $34,000. There was no loss of life during the casualty or subsequent salvage operations.

Today, the *Cumberland's* wreckage is intermingled with that of the *Henry Chisholm*, wrecked on the same site 21 years later, and not far from that of the *George M. Cox*, wrecked in 1933. Collectively these three wrecks, the *Cumberland*, the *Chisholm* and the *Cox*, have caused Rock of Ages Reef to become popularly known as the "reef of the Three C's."

Sidewheeler <u>CUMBERLAND</u> is the only vessel of her type wrecked at Isle Royale. (Canal Park Marine Museum Collection)

HENRY CHISHOLM (1880-1898)

While scouring the waters of western Lake Superior for her lost schooner-barge tow, the wooden steamer *Henry Chisholm* fetched up on Rock of Ages Reef on October 20, 1898, in virtually the same place as the *Cumberland*. Their wreckage is jumbled together in over 100 feet of water.

The *Henry Chisholm* was but one player in an 1898 end-of-season wreck quartet. Only three days before the *Chisholm's* loss, schooner *John Jewett* stranded in nearby Grace Harbor. A month later the steamer *Osceola* stranded outside of Mott Island, and the *Harlem* stranded outside Siskiwit Bay. *John Jewett*, *Osceola*, and *Harlem* were all salvaged, the *Harlem* nearly a year after her accident. Not so for the *Henry Chisholm*.

Four days before the accident, on October 16, the *Henry Chisholm* completed loading 92,000 bushels of barley for Buffalo and picked up her tow, the *John Martin*, just off the Duluth Entry. The *Martin* carried 1,200,000 board feet of lumber. By late afternoon they were engulfed in foul weather somewhere off Isle Royale and north of Copper Harbor. The storm became so bad that Captain James Lawless of the *Martin* decided, in the interest of safety, to cut the towline and strike out on his own. There was no way to communicate with Captain P.H. Smith of the *Chisholm*, but Smith knew immediately when the line was dropped because the *Chisholm* lurched

ahead, freed of her burden. The two vessels separated, quickly losing sight of one another.

The *Chisholm* plodded along nearly two more days before the storm subsided enough for her to begin an active search for her tow. She began retracing their original course, putting in at Ashland, Wisconsin, to refuel. She resumed searching on the 19th, eventually working north toward Isle Royale, hoping to find the *John Martin* safely sheltered there.

In pre-dawn darkness at about 5 o'clock on October 20, as Captain Smith and Mate Whitsman were below discussing details of the search, the *Henry Chisholm* struck hard. She was under direction of the second mate and had been running at about nine knots, making for the entry to Washington Harbor. The *Chisholm* rapidly took on a four-foot list, settling atop three rock pinnacles with 12 feet of water under her bow and 40 feet below the stern. Pieces of hull planking sprang loose and water poured into the engine room extinguishing her boiler fires.

A hurried damage assessment told Captain Smith there was little hope for his vessel. He ordered Mate Whitsman, along with the second mate, two wheelsmen and a seaman, to take the 18-foot open yawl and make for the Canadian shore to report their situation. These men were spotted the next day by Booth Fisheries Steamer *Hiram R. Dixon* and taken into Port Arthur where they wired the bad news to owner M.A. Bradley in Cleveland.

Shortly after the first small boat left, Captain Smith, the chief engineer, two

Steamer **HENRY CHISHOLM** was originally capable of carrying full sail, but later her masts were reduced and the middle one was removed completely.
(Great Lakes Historical Society Collection)

stewards and six other sailors made for Washington Island to await word from the head office. They took with them nearly all the personal effects of the entire crew as well as the ship's papers. The uninsured *Henry Chisholm* was valued at about $70,000, her cargo at about $45,000. She had been built in 1880 at Cleveland by Thomas Quayle's Sons, an old and reputable shipbuilding firm.

Word of the wreck quickly spread to Duluth and the Keweenaw Peninsula. Captain B.B. Inman assembled a wrecking expedition and set out from Duluth. Captain Walter H. Singer, also of Duluth, proceeded to the scene from Copper Harbor where he had just completed a salvage survey on the *James H. Farwell*, stranded the same day the *Chisholm* left Duluth. Singer's appraisal of the *Chisholm's* situation was gloomy, noting she would likely be added to Lake Superior's long list of victims. Inman put two steam pumps aboard the wreck, but made no headway. He said it might take eight or ten more pumps to refloat the *Chisholm* and then only if the weather held.

On the night of October 24, heavy seas, whipped by 27-mile per hour winds, began developing, eventually driving wreckers from the *Chisholm*. This blow lasted well into the 26th, followed by an equally severe storm on the 29th and 30th. Flotsam spread for miles around the wreck scene, and by Halloween the *Henry Chisholm* had completely broken apart and settled on the bottom.

Meanwhile on October 21, north of Copper Harbor, the steamer *Roman*,

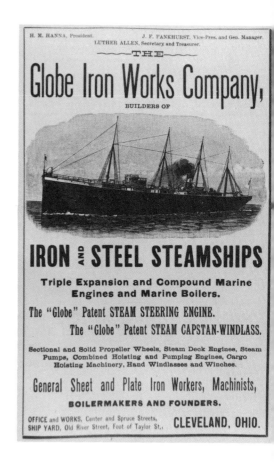

Wreck of the **HENRY CHISHOLM** is clearly marked by her steam engine, built by Globe Iron Works in 1880.
(Author's Collection)

esponding to Captain Lawless' distress calls, took the *John Martin* in tow and headed toward the Soo where the schooner-barge would be repaired.

Interest in the *Henry Chisholm* resurfaced in 1901 when Captain Alexander Sinclair of Duluth mounted a salvage effort. Wreckers, working under Captain Edward England off the *Joseph C. Suit*, managed to raise at least one of the *Chisholm's* boilers and bring it in to the shipyard at Superior, Wisconsin. England's divers also located the steam engine, but at over 100 feet, it was reported beyond their salvage ability.

Sport divers visiting the wreck today are primarily diving the *Henry Chisholm's* two-cylinder steam engine. The engine stands upright in nearly perfect condition at a depth of about 150 feet. The engine was built in 1880 for the *Henry Chisholm* by Cleveland's Globe Iron Works. Engine number 128 was a fore-and-aft, compound engine with 30 and 56-inch cylinders and a 48-inch stroke. The engine stands about 20 feet high with ornate iron work accenting its massive structure. Nearby are the intermingled timbers of the *Chisholm* and *Cumberland*, except for the engine, nearly all that remains of these two distinctively different Great Lakes vessels.

GEORGE M. COX (1901-1933)

More than $80,000 was poured into refitting and rebuilding the old Lake Michigan passenger liner *Puritan* to convert her into the handsome *George M. Cox* just in time for the opening of the Century of Progress Exposition in Chicago. Yet, she didn't last out her first week after re-christening, much less her maiden voyage before becoming the third victim on Rock of Ages Reef. *George M. Cox* added the third and final "C" to the "Reef of the Three C's" on May 27, 1933, opening day of the Exposition.

Built in 1901 at Toledo, Ohio, as the *Puritan* by Craig Shipbuilding Company, this vessel saw a relatively active career on lower Lake Michigan, running between Chicago, Benton Harbor, and St. Joseph with occasional runs up the lake to Mackinac Island. Her owners had her lengthened in 1908 from 235 feet to 270 feet overall, providing additional passenger accommodations and freight space. She was taken over in 1918 by the Navy Department to serve as a troop transport and training vessel, but saw virtually no service because the war ended

Steamer **GEORGE M. COX** in Chicago after she was re-christened. She formerly was the **PURITAN**. (Herman G. Runge Collection Milwaukee Public Library) ⟶

soon afterwards. She was released by the Navy in 1920 and eventually owned by the Michigan Transit Company, successor to the Northern Michigan Transportation Company. She then traded actively until the 1930s depression.

An enterprising vessel owner, shipbuilder, and entrepreneur of New Orleans, George M. Cox, learned of the availability of the *Puritan* and a similar vessel, the *Manitou*, and decided to begin a new transportation service in connection with the Chicago Exposition. Both vessels were purchased by the Isle Royale Transportation Company, Inc. of Arizona and completely refitted, the *Puritan* becoming *George M. Cox*, with a completely new deck of passenger cabins added, and the *Manitou* becoming the *Isle Royale*. It was planned that eventually the *Cox* would become a floating hotel, making only short excursions out of Chicago. The *Isle Royale* would make a passenger and freight run up Lake Michigan and on Lake Superior.

George M. Cox was re-christened by the daughter of the mayor of Chicago in a grand ceremony on the Chicago waterfront on May 25, 1933. The *Cox*, with a new master and crew, left quickly for the Copper Country (Keweenaw Peninsula) on her first trip ever onto Lake Superior. She was welcomed in Michigan at Houghton-Hancock on the Portage Lake Ship Canal early on May 27, then headed northwesterly around the southwest end of Isle Royale toward Thunder Bay. She was carrying primarily crew members and a handful of specially invited guests, personal friends of Mr. Cox and his business associates.

It was a sunny day when the *Cox* left the Canal and set her course. Captain George E. Johnson turned over command to First Mate Arthur Kronk. Late in the afternoon, as the *Cox* approached Isle Royale, Johnson was called back to the bridge because the vessel was about to enter a low-hanging fog bank. They could see the top of Rock of Ages Light house just before they entered the fog. At 5:20 p.m. they clearly heard the fog signal and noted its position relative to the ship. They continued on course until 6:10 p.m. when the fog signal become more distinct.

Captain Johnson's testimony as reported in the Houghton "Daily Mining Gazette" continues the story: "Discovering that we were near abreast of the light, owing to a greater speed than I had anticipated, we received an alarm signal from the Rock of Ages Lighthouse and immediately I put the wheel hard to starboard and steered west for eight minutes. At 6:18, feeling assured we were at least two and one-half miles westward of the lighthouse, I hauled slowly to the northwest in order to get a bearing on Rock of Ages Light."

Captain Johnson then noted that visibility was about a quarter mile, perhaps 1,500 feet, and their speed was about 10 miles per hour Continuing, he said, "We struck the reef at 6:20 p.m. Immediately we gave signals to stop the engine and ordered the boats manned and lowered. All lifeboats on the port side were lowered in ten minutes. The boat being so badly listed to port it was impossible to lower the starboard boats. When the boats were well clear of the steamer, we unlashed the rafts from the star board and slipped them across to the port side. All ladies and children, about thirty in number, were placed in the first two boats. When the lifeboats were filled and underway, the motor boat from the lighthouse took some of the lifeboats in tow, and in doing so made good progress in landing passengers at the lighthouse. At 7:30 p.m. all passengers and crew were off the steamer."

Before abandoning ship, the *Cox* managed to send out an S O S which was picked up by freighter *Morris B. Tremaine*, which was in the vicinity. The *Tremaine* set course to the wreck scene and stood by about eight miles off the lighthouse to take on the few injured persons and transport them to the hospital in Fort William. Going with the injured were the ship's nurse, Adeline Keeling, and owner, George M. Cox. The most severe injuries were a broken leg and burns from hot grease that spilled from french fries being prepared for the evening meal.

U.S. Coast Guardsmen aboard the Cutter *Crawford* set out from Two Harbors, Minnesota, within twenty minutes of the S O S. Crews also responded from Coast Guard stations at Grand Marais, Minnesota, and the Portage Ship Canal on Michigan's Keweenaw Peninsula. Because of the skill of the *Cox's* crew and the alertness of Rock of Ages Lightkeeper John F. Soldenski, the largest mass rescue in the history of Lake Superior shipwrecks was accomplished in an orderly manner. Some 120 persons quickly became guests of the Soldenskis, most housed on the spiraling staircase while, throughout the night, a few were forced to take turns standing outside at the base of the tower.

George M. Cox posed for newspaper photographs in Houghton following loss of his namesake ship and a substantial investment.

(Author's Collection)

Listing sharply from her grounding, <u>**GEORGE M. COX**</u>
teetered precariously on Rock of Ages reef for months
before finally breaking apart and sinking
on both sides of the reef.

(Thunder Bay Historical Society Collection)

Derrick barge **STRATHBUOY** works at salvaging life
boats from **GEORGE M. COX** in June 1933.
(Herman G. Runge Collection, Milwaukee Public Library)

The following morning all were transferred to the Singer Hotel on Washington Island. Later, they were transported to Houghton.

Ship's Nurse Adeline Keeling recalled her own experiences at the time of the accident: "There was one heavy thud, followed by a series of crashes. The passengers were at dinner at the time. I saw a heavy buffet slide across the floor and crash into tables and a partition. I was in my stateroom and was thrown against a door and stunned. The stewardess, Beatrice Cote, helped me to my feet, and was herself knocked down in the second crash. She injured her back. There was no panic, but the steamer listed heavily to port and the passengers and crew rushed to starboard."

Subsequent survey of the *Cox's* damage revealed that her bottom was literally torn out. Her engine was jolted from its mount and her hull split along the keel for a considerable length. It appeared the *Cox* would eventually break amidships where she rested on the reef and sink. It took more than a month before she broke, and not until an October storm was she completely submerged. However, many items had been removed over the summer and stored at the Booth Fisheries dock in Port Arthur.

The casualty hearing was held in Houghton at the Douglass House with many of the officers, crew and passengers testifying. Considerable conflicting testimony was heard about the course that should have been set from the Portage Canal to Isle Royale and about who was actually in charge of the vessel at the moment of impact. At one point the allegations became more animated: after an afternoon of particularly damning testimony against First Mate Kronk, the verbal battle continued into the Douglass House lobby where it errupted into a shouting match between Kronk and the company's manager, Mark L. Gilbert. Kronk managed to get in the first swing, but the only blow struck was squarely delivered by Gilbert. Bystanders separated the two before either might or right won out. Ultimately, Captain Johnson and Kronk were stripped of their licenses for "reckless navigation in fog and inattention to duty."

There are no more passenger liners like the *George M. Cox* operating on the Great Lakes. Only shipwrecks and museum vessels are left to remind us of this once-grand way to travel on the Great Lakes.

AMERICA (1898-1928)

There are few ships on Lake Superior now, or in the memories of those who live along the north shore between Duluth-Superior and Thunder Bay, that are recalled with more genuine affection than the steamer *America*. Many lost an old and dear friend when the *America* stranded in the North Gap of Isle Royale just off Washington Harbor on June 7, 1928.

The *America* was built in 1898 to operate primarily as a day-excursion boat between various Michigan ports and Chicago. She was originally 164.6 feet long, but was lengthened in 1910-11 to 182.6 feet, adding twelve additional staterooms forward of the engine room and smoke stack. She handled as many as 1,200 excursionists at a time while in service on Lake Michigan, but never reached that number under veteran master Jacob F. Hector after arriving at Duluth in 1902. The new owner, Booth Fisheries, had invested more than $15,000 in improving the *America* before bringing her up to Duluth. Among their new ship's assets were her steel hull and speed of 18 miles per hour; many of the local Booth vessels were wooden hulled and slow, the cause of numerous complaints.

One thing that no shipwright can build into a vessel is promptness; that is the master's responsibility. Captain Hector and the *America* made their appointed rounds on time despite treacherous weather and a rugged shoreline route. There were many hazards and unforeseen circumstances lying ahead of the *America* each day, but she was nearly always on schedule and had little more than a half dozen incidents in her 27-season Lake Superior career, which included more than 2,000 round trips up the shore, almost half a million miles. Rocks, reefs, fog, snow, ice, and smoke from distant forest fires all combined against anyone who sailed the north shore. So skillfully did Hector master the *America* that he became known everywhere along his route as the "Fog King." He was hardly a cold and lordly master though; just half an hour out of port, he'd have met all the passengers, calling most by first names before the next stop.

Captain Hector remained in command of the *America* into the 1910 season when his health began to fail. He died later that summer. From his position as first mate, Captain Edward C. "Indian" Smith took over the *America*. No finer successor could have been named. Indeed, the old master's warmth with passengers and crew were retained as was his passion for promptness. Smith was said to know the *America* and the route so well that he "could smell his way along the north shore." Many noted his ability to navigate in fog: he could blow the *America's* beautiful steam whistle, listen for the echo, and know exactly when to adjust his course and speed. The *America* would soon emerge alongside a skiff, hand down mail and groceries, then disappear into the fog. On the return trip she'd stop again to pick up passengers, mail and kegs and boxes of fish.

The *America's* last season began as many before it: she was among the first vessels to leave port and certainly the first to bring the

The United States and Dominion Transportation Company
operated Booth Fisheries steamer **AMERICA**
on Lake Superior.
(Canal Park Marine Museum Collection)

In this 1920s postcard the steamer <u>AMERICA</u> leaves Duluth Harbor
for Isle Royale and Lake Superior's North Shore.
(Canal Park Marine Museum Collection)

Steamer America, Belle Isle, Isle Royale, Mich.

Vacationers on Belle Isle welcome steamer
AMERICA in this postcard view. She serviced
all the resorts on Isle Royale.
(Canal Park Marine Museum Collection)

An old wood cut of steamer **AMERICA** shows her
wireless antenna strung between her fore and
aft masts. She was one of the first vessels operating
on Lake Superior to carry wireless.
(Author's Collection)

52

ong winter's news up the shore. Grand
Marais, Minnesota, citizens once again
presented Captain Smith with a fine new hat
as skipper of the first vessel into their pictur-
esque harbor. There were no signs that this
would be the *America's* final season.

On her last trip steamer *America* cleared
Duluth Entry on June 6, 1928, touching at
her usual ports enroute to Thunder Bay. The
next day in early morning darkness she headed toward Isle Royale from Grand Marais to
drop off a number of passengers so they
wouldn't have to wait out the trip to Port
Arthur and around the northeastern tip of
the island before landing at their Washington Harbor destination. In all, 48 people
remained aboard when the *America* slipped
away from the dock in Washington Harbor.
Captain Smith turned over command to First
Mate John Wick and retired to his stateroom.
Only a short time later the *America* thudded
over a reef, tearing a small hole in her
bottom. At first Engineer Frank McMillin
thought the pumps would keep her afloat,
but he soon changed his mind. The captain
rushed to the wheelhouse and ordered the
crew to awaken the passengers and prepare
the lifeboats. He then ordered Wheelsman
Fred Nelson to put her hard astarboard
toward a small gravel beach in the North
Gap. About 30 yards offshore, she snagged a
second reef which held her fast.

Wheelsman Nelson later described the
event: "We were outbound in Washington
Harbor about a half mile from the dock
when the ship struck a reef. This caused a
loud noise which awakened most of the crew
and passengers. Those who were not up

Captain Edward C. "Indian" Smith becomes friends
quickly with two young ladies enroute to Isle Royale on
steamer **AMERICA**. Notice fire buckets in foreground.
(Canal Park Marine Museum Collection)

when the crash occurred came on deck when the ship's bell started ringing. Members of the crew went to cabin doors telling passengers and crew of the danger. The boat started sinking slowly. All five of the ship's lifeboats were launched. Members of the crew were assigned to take charge of the boats and everyone was taken off. Capt. Edward C. Smith left on the last boat just before the entire ship was practically under water."

One of the passengers, H.S. Cottier, said, "There was absolutely no confusion aboard the *America* when it became known she had struck a reef. The crew launched five lifeboats within a few minutes and pushed off with the passengers for Washington Island. ...It was my first shipwreck and I was struck with the absolute control the crew had over the situation." He added, "We were taken to Washington Island where Mr. Singer, proprietor of the resort there, made us comfortable."

Subsequent investigation into the cause of the *America's* stranding determined that First Mate John Wick, on his first assignment to the *America* and unfamiliar with the local waters, chose a course too close to shore in the moonlit darkness. He was censured for careless navigation. No other officer shared fault.

The Fort William "Daily Times Journal" carried a most fitting epitaph: "The unfortunate loss of the steamer *America* has, for a time as least, removed from the run between Fort William and Duluth, a boat that has served the public at the head of the lakes in good stead for over a quarter of a century.

In the top photograph the <u>**AMERICA's**</u> engine room crew pose patriotically in their place of work. In the bottom photograph one of the <u>**AMERICA's**</u> "black gang" poses in the hot, dark, and dirty boiler room.

(Horace LaClair Photograph)

Steamer **<u>AMERICA</u>** took a beating during the winter,
but tourists at Washington Harbor enjoyed exploring
the wreck the following summer.
(Canal Park Marine Museum Collection)

"While connection with Duluth had been maintained by the passenger boats of the Canada Steamship Line, originally the Northern Navigation Company, it was the *America* which did the local, routine work along the north shore, poking her nose into every little harbor on the coast line and keeping communication between the mainland and Isle Royale uninterrupted. While the *Hamonic* was sailing majestically from point to point, the *America* was serving all the places enroute. She was like the local train which unloads its freight at every unimportant siding, past which the stately express train glides as if it never existed."

There was immediate hope of salvaging the *America* by Captain Cornelius O. Flynn of Duluth, who surveyed the wreck. But his hopes vanished with the onset of the 1930s depression. He acquired ownership of the *America* through the courts, however, and passed it along to his son. An attempt was made in the 1960s to raise the *America* for a tourist attraction at Duluth, but a number of problems halted the effort.

Today, the *America* is very popular among scuba divers because she is relatively intact, easy to find, and in relatively shallow water. Still, one diver has been lost on the wreck. Excursionists traveling from Grand Portage to Isle Royale pass over the *America* enroute, often catching a glimpse of this once fine passenger and package freight steamer. The *America* is as popular now as she was then.

The wreck of the **AMERICA** provided tourists with excitement even after loss, in 1928. (Canal Park Marine Museum Collection)

57

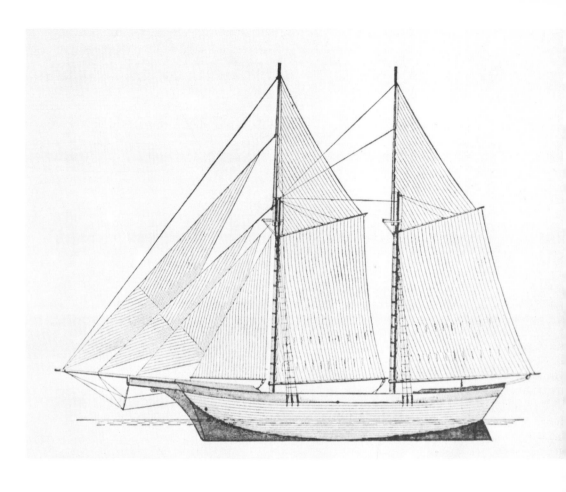

A full-rigged scow schooner similar to the <u>YOU TELL</u>, lost at Isle Royale in 1872, one of several "known lost, but still missing" shipwrecks.
(Author's Collection)

OTHER SHIPWRECKS

Isle Royale National Park's 10 major shipwrecks are just a small part of the 350 known total losses on Lake Superior and represent only a partial picture of the island's overall marine casualty history. There have been dozens of Isle Royale shipwrecks in which the ships did not become total losses. There are also several vessels known to have been wrecked at Isle Royale which have not been discovered or rediscovered in recent times. In addition to these, there are many submerged or partially submerged vessels which were simply abandoned. Finally, there are a number of large marine artifacts such as anchors, rudders, and hull plating whose sources have not yet been positively identified.

In researching these "other" shipwrecks or casualties, one develops a particular fondness for the abandoned vessels because their histories often seem more personal. Yet, it is the "known lost, but still missing" vessels which have the captivating essence of mystery about them.

Here are capsulized glimpses of some of these still missing vessels which may some day become part of the next-to-last chapter on Isle Royale shipwrecks. Already mentioned were the schooner *Northern Belle*, lost in 1884-85 at Wright Island, and the tug *George Hand*, lost off Little Schooner Island in 1886.

The scow schooner *You Tell*, built at Detroit in 1866, is the oldest known loss and the only one of her type wrecked at Isle Royale. This 56-foot vessel was wrecked in an October 1872 gale while anchored in Washington Harbor where it literally went to pieces.

Fire destroyed another 56-foot wooden vessel, the *John A. Styninger*, at Grace Harbor in November 1915 while she was returning from commercial fishing in Siskiwit Bay. She had been built only two years earlier at Bay City, Michigan.

Fire also destroyed the 48-foot gas yacht *Peggy Bee*, docked at the Singer Hotel dock on Washington Island, in August 1928. She was built in 1917 at Albany, New York, and was owned by Homer W. Bleckley of Buffalo.

Fire consumed to the water line the 21-foot plywood cabin cruiser *Fingerling* in July 1948 while the Herbert Montgomery family of Chicago was fishing off Blake Point.

The *Dagmar*, a small, wooden freight vessel, ran ashore on a foggy June night in 1935 and slipped into deeper water one mile northeast of Chippewa Harbor before sunrise the following day. The 45-foot boat had been built in 1914 near Beaver Bay, Minnesota, by her first owner, Christian Ronning. She was owned by Brazelle Motor Freight Co. of Grand Marais, Minnesota, when lost.

In November 1874 a mackinaw sail boat traveling from the Keweenaw Peninsula to Silver Islet crashed ashore in a blinding snow storm near the abandoned Epidote Mine. Two of the three on board, the McGuire brothers, survived while their companion perished with the boat. The brothers eventually made their way to Island Mine after a meandering journey of several days. This type of boat was very common on the Lakes in the

19th century, but is virtually extinct today except for reproductions. The final chapter on Isle Royale shipwrecks has yet to be written; it may never be written, at least not until all shipping ceases on Lake Superior.

Windlass and capstan arrangement similar to that salvaged in the 1960s from the **MONARCH**
(Author's Collection)

REFERENCES

These shipwreck histories were compiled from a great many sources. For example, the account of the *Kamloops'* loss was derived over a 20-year period. The quest involved a dozen major interviews in Sarnia, Southampton, Thunder Bay, Duluth, Minneapolis, Grand Marais, and at Isle Royale, as well as extensive book and periodical searches resulting in more than 300 pages of correspondence, notes, and clippings. Below is a brief list of references and institutional sources pertaining not only to these Isle Royale shipwrecks, but to shipwrecks elsewhere on Lake Superior and the other Great Lakes. Many of the books and periodicals can be found in public libraries in port cities around the lakes or obtained through interlibrary loan.

Books: James P. Barry, *Ships of the Great Lakes: 300 Years of Navigation (1973)*, an excellent overview. James P. Barry, *Wrecks and Rescues of the Great Lakes: A Photographic History (1981)*. Bruce Berman, *Encyclopedia of American Shipwrecks (1974)*. Dana Thomas Bowen, *Shipwrecks of the Lakes (1952)* and two other volumes. Dwight Boyer, *Ghost Ships of the Great Lakes (1968)* and four other volumes. Mac Frimodig, *Shipwrecks off Keweenaw (1974)*. Great Lakes Historical Society, *"Inland Seas,"* quarterly journal. Great Lakes Maritime Institute, *"Telescope,"* bimonthly journal. John O. Greenwood, *Namesakes (Of the Lakes)*, 1930-1955, (1978). John O. Greenwood, *Namesakes (Of the Lakes)*, 1956-1980, (1981) and four other volumes. Francis Ross Holland, Jr., *America's Lighthouses: Their Illustrated History Since 1716*, (1972). Capt. H.C. Inches, *The Great Lakes Wooden Shipbuilding Era* (n.d.). Lake Superior Marine Museum Association of Duluth, *"The Nor'easter,"* bimonthly journal. J.B. Mansfield, editor, *History of the Great Lakes* in two volumes (1899). *Merchant Vessels of the United States*, annual since 1867. John M. Mills, *Canadian Coastal and Inland Steam Vessels*, 1809-1930, (1979), an excellent source for data on Canadian vessels and U.S. crossovers. Grace Lee Nute, *Lake Superior (1944)*, part of the American lakes series. William Ratigan, *Great Lakes Shipwrecks and Survivals (1977)*. Frederick Stonehouse, *Went Missing: Fifteen Vessels that Disappeared on Lake Superior (1977)* and five other volumes. *U.S. Life-Saving Service Annual Report (1872-1915)*. *U.S. Light-House Board Annual Report (1852-1903)*. Homer D. Wells, Jr. *"History of Accidents, Casualties, and wrecks on Lake Superior,"* typewritten manuscript in files of Canal Park Marine Museum, U.S. Army Corps of Engineers, Duluth Area Office (1938). A Winklemann, *Shipping Casualties Resulting in Total Loss on the Great Lakes, 1870-1970*, (c. 1970), for Canadian registered ships only. Dudley Witney, *The Lighthouse (1975)* for Canadian lighthouses. Wisconsin Marine Historical Society, *"Soundings"* (Occasional). Dr. Julius F. Wolff, Jr., *The Shipwrecks of Lake Superior (1979)*, the only comprehensive listing of over 1,200 wrecks on Lake Superior. Additionally, the two works of

Lawrence Rakestraw, *Historic Mining on Isle Royale (1965)* and *Commercial Fishing on Isle Royale (1968)* provide excellent background and companion reading for *Above and Below*.

Institutions: Canadian Coast Guard of Ottawa, Ont. Institute for Great Lakes Research at Bowling Green State University in Bowling Green, Ohio. Chicago Historical Society of Chicago. Dossin Great Lakes Museum on Belle Isle in Detroit, Mich. Marquette County Historical Society in Marquette, Mich. Michigan Technological University Library Archives (Chynoweth Collection) in Houghton, Mich. Milwaukee Public Library (Herman G. Runge Collection) in Milwaukee, Wisc. Public Archives of Canada in Ottawa, Ont. Public Archives of Ontario in Toronto, Ont. The National Archives & Records Service in Washington, D.C. Thunder Bay Historical Society in Thunder Bay, Ont. U.S. Army Corps of Engineers' Canal Park Marine Museum in Duluth, Minn. University of Detroit Marine Collection in Detroit, Mich.

ACKNOWLEDGEMENT

Sincere appreciation for their assistance and cooperation goes to many individuals and institutions: particularly to Carol Maass, Bruce Weber and Ken Vrana of Isle Royale National Park; to editor Norma Lee Stuart for her major contribution in preparing the final manuscript; to Roy Oberg and the Holte, Johnson, Sivertson, Edisen, Martin, Farmer, Rude and Merritt families of Isle Royale, who welcomed me on many occasions; to Merlyn C. "Red" Dahl, Doc Fleming and Kit Kenney, who introduced me to the Island they had known in the 1950s. Special thanks to my wife Cindi and daughter Rachael, who allowed me to spend so many hours away from home in research, writing and travel to the "wilderness port" of Lake Superior.

T. R. H.

* Special Note: Lighthouse lenses made by the Fresnel Company of France were classified into "orders" ranging from one to six. The order indicates the relative magnitude and intensity or size of the light. A "first order" lens assembly stands over 7½ feet high and six feet in diameter while a "sixth order" lens measures only 16 inches tall.

The **GLENLYON**, like Isle Royale's other shipwrecks, is now a popular attraction for experienced scuba divers.

(NPS/Submerged Cultural Resources Unit)

ISLE ROYALE LIGHTS

	Tower height	Operated
Blake Point	20 ft	1917 - present
Isle Royale (Menagerie Is)	55	1875 - present
Passage Island	37	1882 - present
Rock of Ages	117	1908 - present
Rock Harbor	50	1855 - 1859
		1874 - 1879

ISLE ROYALE SHIPWRECKS

			Ft. long	Depth
Algoma	Can. passenger steamer	1883 - 1885	262	10 - 100
America	U.S.A. package freighter	1898 - 1928	183	2 - 80
Henry Chisholm	U.S.A. bulk freighter	1880 - 1898	265	20 - 140
Chester A. Congdon	U.S.A. bulk freighter	1907 - 1918	532	50 - 200
George M. Cox	U.S.A. passenger steamer	1901 - 1933	259	10 - 100
Cumberland	Can. passenger steamer	1871 - 1877	204	20 - 140
Emperor	Can. bulk freighter	1910 - 1947	525	30 - 175
Glenlyon	Can. bulk freighter	1893 - 1924	328	15 - 60
Kamloops	Can. package freighter	1924 - 1927	250	175 - 260
Monarch	Can. package freighter	1890 - 1906	240	10 - 80

NOTES